GOD

By Alan Watts

Book I in the Illustrated Series

THE ESSENCE OF ALAN WATTS

ALAN WATTS" . . . has provided a series
of sensitively illustrated jewel-books for
the searching spirits of this century. . . ."
—Joseph Campbell

CELESTIAL ARTS
Millbrae, California

First Printing, July, 1974
Second Printing, January, 1975
Made in the United States of America

Cover photo of Alan Watts by Margo Moore
Photo on page 16 by Richard Borst

Library of Congress Cataloging in Publication Data

Watts, Alan Wilson, 1915-1973
    God.

    (His The essence of Alan Watts, v.1)
    1.   God.I. Title.
B945.W321 1974 vol.1 [BT102] 191s [291.2'1]
ISBN 0-912310-75-8   74-13648

THE STORY OF ALAN WATTS

For more than twenty years Alan Watts earned a reputation as the foremost interpreter of Eastern philosophies to the West. Beginning at the age of 20, when he wrote *The Spirit of Zen*, he developed an audience of millions who were enriched by his offerings through books, tape recordings, radio, television, and public lectures.

He wrote 25 books, each building toward a personal philosophy that he shared, in complete candor and joy, with his readers and listeners throughout the world. They presented a model of individuality and self-expression that can be matched by few contemporaries. His life and work reflect an astonishing adventure: he was editor, Anglican priest, graduate dean, broadcaster, and author-lecturer. He had fascinations for cooking, calligraphy, singing, and dancing. He held fellowships from Harvard University and the Bollingen Foundation and was Episcopal Chaplain at Northwestern University. He became professor and dean of the American Academy of Asian Studies in San Francisco, made the television series "Eastern Wisdom and Modern Life" for the National Educational Television, and served as visiting consultant to many psychiatric institutes and hospitals. He traveled widely with students in Japan

Born in England in 1915, Alan Watts attended King's School Canterbury, served on the Council of the World Congress of Faiths (1936–38), and came to the United States in 1938. He held a Master's Degree in Theology from Seabury-Western Theological Seminary and an Honorary D.D. from the University of Vermont in recognition of his work in Comparative Religion.

Alan Watts died in 1973. *The Essence of Alan Watts*, a series of nine books in the unique *Celestial Arts* format, includes edited transcripts by his wife Mary Jane Watts of videotaped lectures that were produced by his friend, Henry Jacobs, and filmed by his son, Mark Watts, in the last years of his life.

Imagine the world coming suddenly out of nothing. Close your eyes and listen and you will hear silence and then sounds coming out of that silence. Now use your eyes and see light, shape, form coming at you as a vibration that is proceeding out of space.

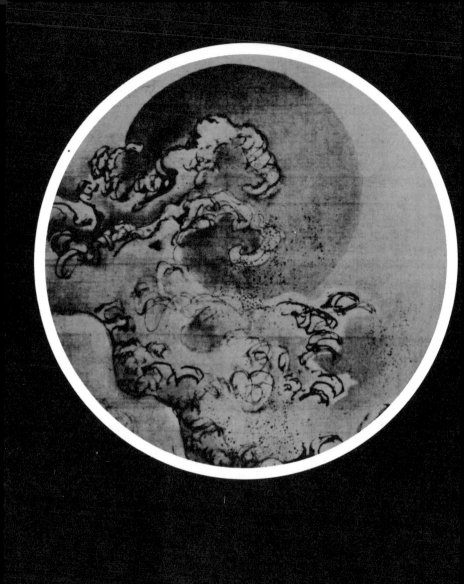

Our logic resists such concepts because common sense tells us we can't get something out of nothing. Normally we think of all the energetic manifestations of this universe as coming out of the past; the things that *were* here are producing the things that *are* here now. But I want you to look at it the other way so that you can see the whole world starting now instead of in the past, and the past as a kind of echo fading away into memory, like the wake of a ship that trails across the water and then fades out. But the wake is started by the ship in the present. In the same way, I am moving on to the uncommonsensical idea of the world as a production of energy that is beginning right now and is coming out of the nothing that we variously call space and silence.

How on earth could that happen? The usual explanation is that the world is being created by God. In Christian theology it is said that God creates the world out of nothing. I want to emphasize the point, in all fairness to Catholic, Islamic, and Jewish doctrine, that it doesn't merely teach that God once upon a time started the world and set it going like you would wind up a machine and then leave it alone. These religions teach that God is always creating the world out of nothing and willing it by his divine energy into being at this moment.

Now the difficulty for most of us—especially for educated people—in the modern world is that the old-fashioned idea of God has become incredible or implausible. In church or in synagogue, we seem to be addressing a royal personage. The layout looks like a royal court. There is some sort of throne, and we address prayers and requests to the being represented by the alter, throne, or tabernacle as if that being were a king and were causing this universe in his royal, omnipotent, and omniscient wisdom.

But then, when we take a look through our telescopes and microscopes or when we just look at nature, we have a problem. Because the idea of God that we get from the holy scriptures, the Bible, the Koran, doesn't quite seem to fit the world around us in just the same way you wouldn't ascribe a composition by Stravinsky to Bach. The style of God venerated in church, mosque, and synagogue seems completely different from the style of the natural universe. It's so hard to conceive the author of the one as the author of the other.

Furthermore, it strikes most intelligent people that our traditional religious ideas of God are primitive. It seems naive to think that this universe could have been authored by a sort of old gentleman who lives far above the stars in heaven, seated on a golden throne and adored by legions of angels. That is a concept unworthy of the sort of universe modern science has revealed to us.

I have a picture of God. A friend of mine photographed a statue of him in a church just south of Oaxaca in Mexico. It shows a primitive Indian-Catholic image of God the Father wearing a triple crown like the Pope, only he's rather young and handsome. He's not like the old, gray-bearded man. This is a serious Christian idol of God the Father Almighty. This is what has become implausible.

But also for many people it has become implausible that the root of the universe, which the theologian Paul Tillich calls the *ground of being*, can be in some way a person to whom we can relate in the same way that we relate to other people—a person who cares about us.

Jesus said, "Five sparrows are sold for a farthing. But yet not one of them falls to the ground without the Father knowing it. So realize that you are of more value than many sparrows." In other words, God cares a great deal more about you. But it just baffles our imagination that there could be this sort of person, who cares about each one of us, who is totally aware of every single thing that we are and that we do and, by virtue of being aware of us, creates us.

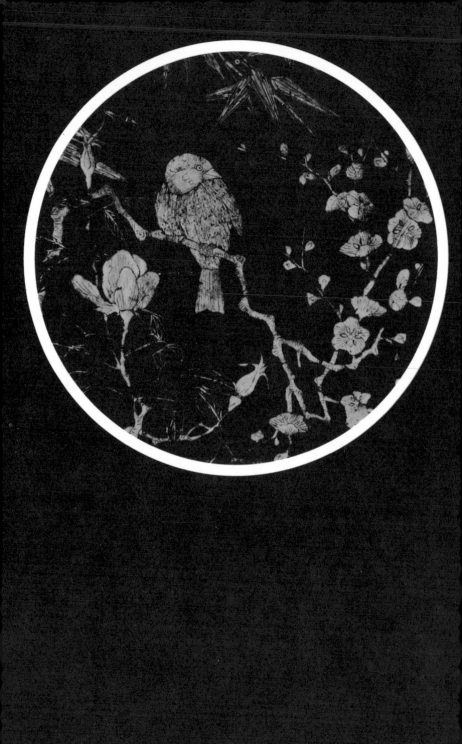

Of course, one thing that is difficult about the idea is that it's embarrassing. We do not feel comfortable if we are watched all the time by an infinitely intelligent judge. Imagine you are a child in school and you're working at some exercise and the teacher walks behind your desk and looks at what you're doing. Even if you like the teacher very much, you feel put down by being watched; it makes you self-conscious and awkward. Many people opt for atheism for the same reason, because they don't want the uncomfortable feeling that they're being watched all the time. It's awkward. And if I were God I wouldn't do it. I wouldn't want to embarrass my creatures in that way, so I would leave them alone for a lot of the time.

The kind of god that people worship is, of course, an attempt to imagine an absolutely perfect human being. But it's a very poor attempt. For example, Jesus taught that if somebody sins against you, forgive him. His disciples asked, "How many times do you forgive him?" And Jesus answered, "Ninety and nine times," *always* forgive somebody who sins against you. But notice, that what is required of a saint—a saint is always forgiving—is not required of God. God will not forgive you unless you apologize, and you have to grovel on the ground if you've committed what the Catholic church calls a mortal sin. You have to come to God in a state of great penitence and if you don't you are liable to be confined in the dungeons of the court of Heaven, commonly known as Hell, for always and always and always.

Now, I don't think that's a very nice kind of fellow. You wouldn't invite that sort of God to dinner. He would embarrass everybody! When God would look at you, you would feel you were being seen through and through, and that all your awful past, all your falseness, would be completely perceptible to him. And though he understood it and forgave it he would nonetheless make you feel absolutely terrible. You just wouldn't want that sort of company at dinner.

You may think it's frivolous of me to describe such a situation, but don't forget the pictorial image of God that people have in the backs of their minds. Even if you're a very sophisticated philosopher or theologian, that primitive pictorial image has a very strong influence on your feelings about religion, about the universe, and about yourself. This is the reason that the traditional idea of God has become implausible to many people.

Modern Protestant theologians, and even some Catholics, have been talking recently about the death of God and about the possibility of a religionless religion, a religion which does not involve belief in God. What would become of the Gospel of Jesus Christ if it were shown that Jesus' own belief in God was unnecessary and invalid? What would remain of his teachings? Of his ideas about caring for other human beings, about social responsibility and so on. I think that would be a pretty wishy-washy kind of religion. If you're going to say that this life is fundamentally nothing but a pilgrimage from the maternity ward to the crematorium and that's it, baby, you've had it, I think that indicates a singular lack of imagination. I would like to look at the death-of-God theology in an entirely different way. What is dead is not God but an idea of God, a particular conception of God that has died in the sense of becoming implausible. And I find this a very good thing.

The Greek word in the New Testament for a sin is *antinomic* or *anomia* and that means to miss the point or, as in archery, to miss the mark. And therefore, from the Mosaic Ten Commandments comes the idea that it is a sin, a missing of the point, to substitute an idol for God.

Then, the statue of God I described is an idol. But even those Mexican-Indians, don't seriously confuse that particular image with God. The danger of it is they may think of God in the form of man. But the images that have been made of God out of wood and stone and in painting have never really been taken seriously as actually what God is like. Nobody has confused the actual image of Buddha for the statues commonly seen in the East. Buddha is never identified with a god because Buddha is a human being, and these images are never seriously confused with what they represent any more than a Catholic confuses a crucifix with Jesus Christ.

The images of God that are tangible are not really very dangerous. The dangerous images of God are those that we make, not out of wood and stone, but out of ideas and concepts. Sir Thomas Aquinas, for example, defined God as a necessary being, He who is necessarily. That is a philosophical concept; but that concept is an idol because it confuses God with an idea. Because an idea is abstract it seems much more spiritual than an image made of wood or stone. That's precisely where it becomes deceptive.

Many people think that the Bible is the authentic word of God and they worship the Bible, making it into an idol. They disregard the ironical remark of Jesus to his contemporary Jews, "You search the scriptures daily, for in them you think you have life." And as St. Paul said later, "The letter kills, but the spirit gives life." So whatever you put as an image or an idea in the place of God necessarily falsifies God.

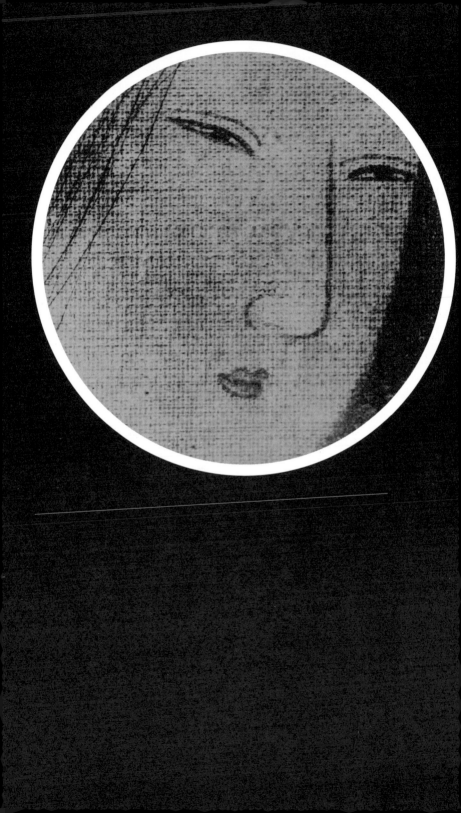

A lot of people say, "I don't think I could face life unless I could believe in a just and loving god." It strikes me that that kind of belief in God is actually expressing a lack of faith. The word belief in Anglo-Saxon comes from the Anglo-Saxon root *lief* which means to wish. So belief really means a strong wish. When you say the creed, "I believe in God, the Father Almighty, maker of heaven and earth and of all things seen and unseen," you are really saying: *"I fervently wish that there exists* God the Father Almighty, creator of heaven and earth, etc." Because, if you really have faith you don't need belief, because faith is an entirely different attitude from belief.

Faith is a state of openness or trust. To have faith is like when you *trust* yourself to the water. You don't grab hold of the water when you swim, if you go stiff and tight in the water you sink. You have to relax. Thusly, the attitude of faith is the very opposite of clinging, of holding on. In other words, a person who is a fanatic in religion, one who simply has to believe in certain propositions about the nature of God and of the universe is a person who has no faith at all—he's holding on tight.

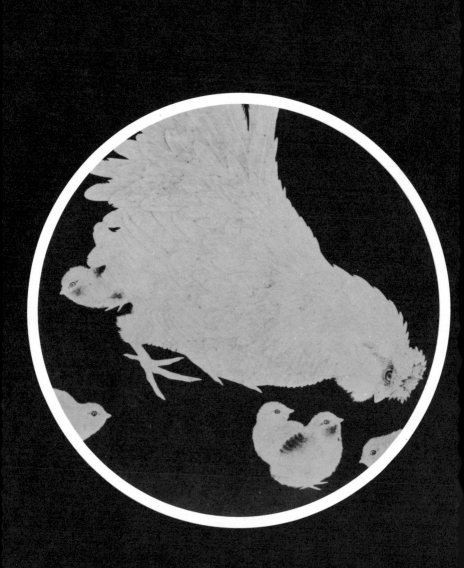

Although Martin Luther made such a thing about faith, he wrote a hymn —in German, *Ein fest Burg ist unser Gott*, "A Mighty Fortress is our God." That's not a hymn of faith! A person of faith doesn't need a fortress; he's not on the defensive.

In the same way, many churches are designed like the royal courts of kings. In the church design called the basilica, which means the court of a basileus or king, the bishop sits at the back in his throne and all his attendant clergy stand around him like his guards in a court. Why is this? A king stands with his back to the wall because he rules by force. And when his subjects and his courtiers approach him they prostrate themselves, they kneel down. Why? Because that's a difficult position from which to start a fight. Are we projecting the image of a frightened king as being the godhead?

The usual Protestant church, on the other hand, looks like a courthouse. The minister wears a black gown as is worn by a judge, and there are pews and pulpits and all the familiar wooden boxes of court furniture. And the minister, like the judge, throws the book at you! He preaches the law laid down in that other idol of God, the Bible. But does God need all that? Is God somebody who takes this aggressive attitude either of the king in court where all the subjects must prostrate, or of the judge who bangs the gavel and interprets the law? This is ridiculous! And a God so conceived is an idol and manifests the absence of faith of all those who worship him because they demonstrate no attitude of trust. They cling to these rules, to these conceptions, and have no fundamental adaptability to life.

You might say that a good scientist has more faith than a religious person, because a good scientist says, "My mind is open to the truth, whatever the truth may turn out to be. I have no preconceptions, but I do have some hypotheses in my mind as to what the truth might be, and I'm going to test them." And the test is to open all the senses to reality and find out what that reality is. But then again, the scientist runs into a problem because he knows that whatever comes to him as reality depends on the structure of his instruments and his senses, and ultimately the structure of his brain. So he has to have faith in his own brain, faith in himself, faith that his physical organism including his mind is indeed reliable and will determine reality, truth—what is.

You have to believe your reason, your logic, your intelligence. You have to have faith in them even though you can't ultimately check on yourself to make certain you're operating properly. It's not like your mind is a radio and can be fixed by screwing in a new connection here and there— you always have to trust.

Therefore, one could say that the highest image of God is the unseen behind the eyes—the blank space, the unknown, the intangible and the invisible. That is God! We have no image of that. We do not know what that is, but we have to trust it. There's no alternative. You can't help trusting it. You've got to.

That trust in a God whom one cannot conceive in any way is a far higher form of faith than fervent clinging to a God of whom you have a definite conception. That conception can easily be wrong and, even if it's right, clinging to it would be the wrong attitude, because when you love someone very much you shouldn't cling to them.

In a New Testament story Mary Magdalene, who loved Jesus very much, is said to have seen him after his resurrection, and she immediately ran to cling to him. And he said, "Do not touch me," but the Greek word *hatir* means to cling to. Don't *cling* to me! Don't cling to anything of the spirit. Don't cling to the water, because the more you grab it the faster it will slip through your fingers. Don't cling to your breath, you'll get purple in the face and suffocate. You have to let your breath out. That's the act of faith, to breathe out, and it will come back. The Buddhist word *nirvana* actually means to breathe out; letting go is the fundamental attitude of faith.

It isn't as if Christians haven't been aware of this. One of the most fundamental sourcebooks of Christian spirituality, *Theologia Mystica*, was written in the sixth century by an Assyrian monk, Dionysius Exiguus. It is a very strange document, because it explains that the highest knowledge of God is through what he calls in Greek *agnostos*, which means unknowing. One knows God most profoundly, the most truly, in not knowing God.

Just as your sight comes out of an unseen, so when you know that you don't know, you really know. You really know, because realizing that you don't know is a state of mind in which you have let go of your efforts to grasp life with your intellect.

The Seven Secret Sayings of God

1 Before [a] the beginning when God created the heaven and the earth, and the earth was without form, and void: and darkness was upon the face of the deep, God said [b] I AM THAT. And it is so.

2 Also, being in eternity which is neither linear nor sequential, where all is now-ever, God said, YOU MUST DRAW THE LINE SOMEWHERE. And it was drawn.

3 But it was no dreary straight line or flat wall, for God then said, HAVE A BALL. And there was a ball, in the image whereof all stars and planets came to be formed.

4 Thereupon God said, THERE ARE TWO SIDES TO EVERYTHING. And there are: inside and the outside, the dense and the spacious, the right and the wrong, the left and the taken, for, as it is written, [c] One shall be taken, and the other left.

5 And God said, IT MUST BE IN TIME. And thereafter it was, is, and will be, for as it is written again, [d] As it was in the beginning is now, and ever shall be, through all ages of ages. Amen.

6 And forthwith God said, SPACE IT OUT. Whereupon it came to pass that, beside this and that and now and then, there is also here and there.

7 And God beheld [e] how firm a foundation this was and said unto himself, GET LOST. And there you are.

[a] Gen. 1.1-2.
Ps. 33.6
Acts. 14.15

[b] Ex. 3.14
Jno. 8.58

[c] Mat. 24.40-41

[d] Lit.St. John Chrys.

[e] Hymn 564.